MISSION CONTAMINATION

Scotland

Edited By Kelly Reeves

First published in Great Britain in 2019 by:

Young Writers
Remus House
Coltsfoot Drive
Peterborough
PE2 9BF
Telephone: 01733 890066
Website: www.youngwriters.co.uk

All Rights Reserved
Book Design by Jenni Harrison
© Copyright Contributors 2019
SB ISBN 978-1-78896-862-1
Printed and bound in the UK by BookPrintingUK
Website: www.bookprintinguk.com
YB0408E

FOREWORD

Young Writers was created in 1991 with the express purpose of promoting and encouraging creative writing. Each competition we create is tailored to the relevant age group, hopefully giving each student the inspiration and incentive to create their own piece of work, whether it's a poem, mini saga or a short story. We truly believe that seeing their work in print gives students a sense of achievement and pride in their work and themselves.

Our Survival Sagas series aimed to challenge both the young writers' creativity and their survival skills! One of the biggest challenges, aside from dodging diseased hordes and avoiding the contagion, was to create a story with a beginning, middle and end in just 100 words!

Inspired by the theme of contamination, whether from a natural mutation, a chemical attack or a man-made experiment gone wrong, their mission was to craft tales of fear and redemption, new beginnings and struggles of survival against the odds. As you will discover, these students rose to the challenge magnificently and we can declare *Mission Contamination* a success.

The mini sagas in this collection are sure to set your pulses racing and leave you wondering with each turn of the page: are these writers born survivors?

CONTENTS

Broughton High School, Edinburgh

Anya Clark (13)	1
Ross Williamson (12)	2
Florence Alice Wilson (12)	3
Carson Roberts (14)	4
Daniel Harcus (13)	5
Ruth Macdonald (13)	6
Taylor Sutherland (12)	7
Niall Geany (12)	8
Sandy Jackson (12)	9
Jude Suttie (12)	10
Rudi Allan Molotnikov (13)	11
Greig McVicar (12)	12

Dalkeith High School, Dalkeith

Naina Singh (13)	13
Joshua Lothian (14)	14
Ronnie Yilmaz Simsek (13)	15
Scott Saunders	16
Sophie Peters (13)	17

Lenzie Academy, Lenzie

Orla Muir (14)	18
Emma Coffey (13)	19
Evan Hunter (13)	20
Alvita Tumwijukye (13)	21
Kirsty Dunbar (13)	22
Charles Lin (13)	23
Abbie McGale (12)	24
Kayla Ormiston (12)	25
Lucy Brear (12)	26
Grant Morrison (13)	27

Rory Stuart Slorance (14)	28
Eva Cameron (13)	29
Calvin Williamson (13)	30
Angus Lavy (13)	31
Lee Cairns (13)	32
Emmanuel Mersha (13)	33
Eva Coleman (12)	34
Rebecca Griffiths (13)	35
Steven Murphy (13)	36
Sam Street (14)	37
Safa Hady (13)	38
Angus John Davie (13)	39
Hannah Campbell (12)	40
Ryan Murray (12)	41
Cameron McIntyre (13)	42
Erica Wright (12)	43
Rhia Lotay (12)	44
Victoria Elena Wilson (12)	45
Molly Rush (12)	46
Angelina Vignal (12)	47
Greg Duncan (13)	48
Stewart Forrest (14)	49
Erin Leia Galloway (13)	50
Bethyn Lyall (12)	51
Ewan O'Hara (13)	52
Aisha Ali (13)	53
Hamish Grant Robertson (12)	54
Connor McKinnon (13)	55
Maryam Mian (12)	56
Rebecca Howie (13)	57
Adam Farrel (12)	58
Oliver Leo Barrie (12)	59
Ross Cunningham (13)	60
Kayleigh McKeown (12)	61
Cameron Borthwick (12)	62

Speyside High School, Aberlour

Campbell Robertson (12)	63
Emma Nicoll (12)	64
Molly Bailey (12)	65
Chelsea Hewitt (13)	66
Lucy Grant (13)	67
Jasmine Mears (13)	68
Luca Iannetta (12)	69
Connor Spence (13)	70
Mackenzie Duthie (12)	71
Ethan Thomson (13)	72
Nancy Sunshine Stewart (12)	73
Aimee Anne Hay (12)	74
Alexis Stuart (13)	75
Jake Urquhart (13)	76
Edward Kendrick (13)	77
Olivia Mitchell (12)	78
Thomas Neil Gordon Stepien (12)	79
Martha Morton (12)	80
Katie Jean Walker (12)	81
Josh Shaw-Rose (13)	82
Luke Mackie (13)	83
Leah Wendy McGillivray (12)	84
Ian Forsyth (13)	85
Jamie Boyd (12)	86
Jessica Knox (12)	87
Catriona Lily Bothwell (12)	88
Jack McConnachie (13)	89
Archie Bain (12)	90
Abbie Ettles (12)	91
Matthew McConachie (12)	92
Keirenza Catriona Garden (13)	93
Millan Ormsby (14)	94
Myles Hardie (12)	95
Ben Charleworth (12)	96
Archie Scott (12)	97
Sarah Robertson (12)	98
Keisha McGill (12)	99
Amanda Watson (12)	100
Cailean Dyer (13)	101
Macy Catherine Furness (13)	102
Ethan McIntosh (12)	103

St George's School For Girls, Edinburgh

Sophie Rachael Reid (16)	104
Molly Mathers (11)	105
Niranjana Gopalakrishnan (16)	106
Heidi Masters (12)	107
Amber Devin (15)	108
Jemima Macaulay (11)	109
Evie McCallum	110
Maira Lakshmy Ratnarajah (12)	111
Samantha Emson	112
Gabriela Wysocka (12)	113
Charlotte Duffin (12)	114
Lindsay Young	115
Lucy Gray (13)	116
Alice Honley (15)	117
Esmé Drummond (12)	118
Rebecca Tidswell (12)	119
Morgan Matthews (11)	120

St Machar Academy, Aberdeen

Kai Dark (12)	121
Ben Thom (13)	122
Leya Shaju (12)	123
Sinead Mayo Conlon (13)	124
Euan Reid (12)	125
Gemma Still (12)	126
Oliwia Wilkosz (13)	127
Drew Kris McDermid (14)	128
Sol Bewley-Lataix (13)	129
Noah Jack (12)	130
Kaitlyn Ellis-Jones (12)	131
Natalia Skowronek (12)	132
Zeniya Elaine Pantcheva (14)	133
Leah Paterson (13)	134
Brandon Lee Booth (13)	135
Michael Claro (13)	136
Dana Pinkovska (12)	137
Jorge Lama (13)	138
Hadyn Milne (13)	139
John Ogston (12)	140
Amanda Suprowicz (13)	141

Auguste Urbonaite (12)	142
Suriya Sivakumar (12)	143
Katie Watson (13)	144
Abbie Ann Shepherd (12)	145
Chloe Fyfe (12)	146
Morgan Glennie (13)	147
Cameron Stewart (12)	148
Billy Swan (13)	149
Kuba Szelagowski (13)	150
Milan Bogacki (12)	151
Erin McDonald (13)	152

Stirling High School, Stirling

Hayley Robinson (12)	153
Abbie Barjoti (12)	154
Ella Caitlin Dempsey (12)	155
George MacLean (12)	156
Scarlett Roy (12)	157
Stephen Kerr (12)	158
Chloe Charlotte Stark (12)	159
Kyle Saunders (12)	160
Jenifer June Gillespie (12)	161
Archie West (12)	162
Melissa Turnbull (12)	163
Alyssa Nash (14)	164
Lauren Graham (12)	165

THE MINI SAGAS

The Bunker

Frightened, cold, trapped. It was just the three of them, Chelsey, Emma and Tim, in an underground bunker, hiding from the gut-wrenching, violent zombies.
"We're safe for now, but they will probably find us soon," Chelsey said, trembling.
"Chelsey, zombies don't have brains, it will take years for them to find us. Tim, how about you look about for some food and water?" said Emma.
"Alright then!" Tim said enthusiastically.
Right then, they could hear the scraping of a foot being dragged across the ground and a growl that could haunt your nightmares.
"Quick, go hide!" yelled Chelsey...

Anya Clark (13)
Broughton High School, Edinburgh

The Plague

Like every day, as Bert entered the playground, everyone ran away from him, shouting, "Bert has the plague!"
Except for one little girl Bert had never seen before. She reached out and grabbed Bert's hand. Everyone whispered, "Dolly has the plague," but she didn't care.
The very next day, she was rushed to hospital, then her friends and family fell ill and the same happened to them. Whatever Dolly and the others had was spreading. Soon, the school and their families were dying, apart from Bert. When he heard, he apologised to everyone, one by one. Then the impossible happened...

Ross Williamson (12)
Broughton High School, Edinburgh

The Chess Infection

It started with a game of strategy, skill and patience, where if you made a mistake, you would be defeated, most likely. It's played in almost silence, with just the occasional sound of footsteps. This game is chess.

The Chess Olympiad is where it started. Most countries were there. The infection started, we think, with one of the English players. The first round, England against Germany, started. The players took their time, taking pieces. Now, the Germans had the chess infection. And so it spread player to player, teammate to teammate, but nobody knew until the last game...

Florence Alice Wilson (12)
Broughton High School, Edinburgh

Subject Twenty-Seven

There were twenty-seven subjects and twenty-six have died, one from suicide and the rest from chemical poisoning to try and get rid of the advanced cancer illness and it's time to use the last test subject.

Day one of the injection in Subject Twenty-Seven, looking okay, heartbeat fine and acting normal. Day two, the subject has passed out and there is no heartbeat. Wait, no, no, the subject has woken up and is breaking the glass and his eyes are becoming really dark. Wait, he's eating Bradley and infecting him with something! I need to find the cure...

Carson Roberts (14)
Broughton High School, Edinburgh

The Day Of The Dead

"Doctor! Doctor!" said a woman, running down the corridor with something wrapped in a blanket.
It was a child. The doctor lay him on the bed in his room, unwrapped the blanket.
"Arghhhhh!" said the doctor.
Something was pulsing under the child's skin. A few hours later, he dropped dead. The doctor put on the news.
"Headlines for today, children have all gone, every last one dead!"
But then out of nowhere, in the corner of his eye, something moved under his skin. He was dead. Everything and everyone was dead.

Daniel Harcus (13)
Broughton High School, Edinburgh

Skeleton Beach

I sat on the busy, rustic sand. The sky became dull, the water murky. Soon, the whole beach was drenched in fish skeletons. Questions started flying through my head. What was happening? Would I die next? All of a sudden, I was the only person left on the beach. Had they died or just run away? I slowly stood up to look around. Suddenly, something was crawling in my ear. *What's happening to me?* Everything around me started moving, colours started changing. *What should I do? When will it all end? Everything is black! Is this the end for me?*

Ruth Macdonald (13)
Broughton High School, Edinburgh

The Last Ten

Max walked in the abandoned barn. He heard a noise behind him, but when he turned around, nothing was there. Suddenly, Max was hit on the back of the head and passed out.

When he woke up, he was on a pile of hay. When he looked up, there was a girl. She wasn't affected! Her name was Ruby. There were only ten humans still alive, the rest were zombies - but now the two humans were in the same place. Suddenly, thunder struck and a hoard of zombies started walking towards them. Max screamed.

Ruby said, "Well, this isn't good..."

Taylor Sutherland (12)
Broughton High School, Edinburgh

An Infestation Of Killer Clowns

It was a cold, rainy night. The leaves were blowing from left to right and there was a weird feeling in the air. Suddenly, in the corner of my eye, I saw a woman running and screaming like she was running away from someone. It looked like a clown was chasing her with a big knife. The jagged knife had blood dripping from the sharp blade. But there wasn't just one, there were millions, more than you could possibly see! Lamp posts were falling, the alarms on the cars were going mental. What was happening? Where did they come from?

Niall Geany (12)
Broughton High School, Edinburgh

Zombie Wars

We had nearly made it to the armed car. We all jumped on in time as John hit the accelerator. There were hundreds of zombies left and right. Suddenly, a zombie jumped on and bit Jim on the arm and he screamed in pain as Jeff shot the zombie in the head.

Jim looked up at me, terrified, and said, trembling, "Kill me, you know you have to."

Jeff passed me the gun and I looked into Jim's eyes. I pulled the trigger and the whole world stopped as the lifeless Jim fell back into the crowds of zombies...

Sandy Jackson (12)
Broughton High School, Edinburgh

Morrisons Monster

I was finishing my work at Morrisons supermarket on Ferry Road, Edinburgh. It was late at night. I was finishing my night shift at 4am on a Thursday night. It was just me and the security guard - that I knew of, anyway. Then some green and yellow insect threw lots of jars of Kenco coffee around the store! One hit the security in the back of his bald, shiny, round head. It knocked him out. It grabbed his feet, pulled him into the kitchen and ripped his insides out of his body. Luckily, I got away and I was not touched.

Jude Suttie (12)
Broughton High School, Edinburgh

A Weird Winter

It was a cold, silent morning. No one else was outside. All I could hear were my own footsteps and all I could see was snow and my own shadow. But then, in the distance, there was a big red truck with bright lights on and a revving engine. It was coming towards me and it looked like it was getting faster. As it came closer, I could see the damage it was doing. It looked like it was killing everyone that it went past. It was coming so fast towards me and suddenly... it went completely blank...

Rudi Allan Molotnikov (13)
Broughton High School, Edinburgh

The Last Patient

Dr Cruz was on his last patient for today. Ever since the virus had mutated, Dr Cruz had had more and more patients. In came the nurse, rolling the patient on a squeaky old wheelchair, his restraints with zero space between him and his chest. When he was finally on the bed, Dr Cruz got to work by making a small puncture in his orangey-green vein. They got out his blood jar and slowly let it ooze into it...

Greig McVicar (12)
Broughton High School, Edinburgh

The Evil Parasite

It's day twelve of the infection being spread and more than half of the world's population has been infected. This parasite must've duplicated itself multiple times to get that far. Me, Katie and Allie are stuck in Katie's house and we're running out of food, but we can't go out or we'll get the infection. When I got water from the kitchen, I saw people banging on the window and it looked like they had the infection. We ran to the back so they wouldn't see us, but it was really quite pointless because they were inside of the house...

Naina Singh (13)
Dalkeith High School, Dalkeith

The Bunker

We are surrounded by the infected in the underground bunker. I can hear the infected screeching and squealing, trying their best to get in, but personally, I know those doors won't last forever. I felt like there was no hope. I felt genuine fear in my body. My heart was beating like an out-of-beat drum, just beating on and on and on, non-stop. Then, suddenly, out of the tiniest gap in the massive steel doors, a minuscule drop, which looked like blue blood, fell into the bunker. I knew from that point, they were in...

Joshua Lothian (14)
Dalkeith High School, Dalkeith

Billy Green

Billy suddenly woke up from a good sleep to look outside and see a giant cloud of green smoke rising up from every drain. Billy saw a little boy touch the smoke and the boy collapsed to the ground. Billy knew he had to get out of town fast. Billy immediately went to his car and drove off to the fields. Billy was driving until he accidentally went over a drain. A cloud of smoke went into his engine and made his engine break down. Now, Billy was stranded. He opened his bonnet as a green cloud of smoke rose...

Ronnie Yilmaz Simsek (13)
Dalkeith High School, Dalkeith

The Shadows

I was running for my life, my heartbeat racing in fear. I was in shock from what I just saw. Joe, you know, the bully from eighth grade? He was being ripped apart, limb from limb. I wanted to curl up into a ball and cry until it was over, but I knew I had to continue running from the horrific horror known as the Shadow Plague.
I made a stop at Sidney's house. I walked in to see a rifle pointed right between my eyes but I knew they were just checking. I closed my eyes. *Bang!* Gunshots...

Scott Saunders
Dalkeith High School, Dalkeith

The Rash

The rash was spreading, pulsing, hurting. We had to get out of the city. We had no choice but to run. It was coming quicker than lightning. It was too strong to stop it. It had killed thousands already. We still had five miles 'til we'd reach the end of the city and it was right behind us. There was a glass dome waiting at the end of the city for us. When we got to the dome, all of us would be safe for two hours until we'd start to suffocate. If we left, we would catch the rash...

Sophie Peters (13)
Dalkeith High School, Dalkeith

Silent Pleads For Help...

"It's okay, boy, it's me..."
Growl! Lucifer was getting extremely unwell. My cat was covered in disgusting lumps. I worried he had caught the infection. It spread like wildfire. Effortless tasks became a life or death situation. We were at rock bottom. Oxygen was low. Would we have to open the bunker? Everyone was terrified.
Cough! Everyone turned. An enormous, oozing lump expanded out of my mother's head. Lumps rapidly multiplied. Soon enough, everyone had them. People became weak and stiff. Falling... Dying. Coughs became whimpers. Whimpers became silent pleas for help. The world flashed before my eyes... *I'm finished.*

Orla Muir (14)
Lenzie Academy, Lenzie

A Shot In The Dark

Stars shimmered in the sky, reflected in pools stained red. Maggots bathed in them. Squirming. Feeding. Breeding. He looked down from the trees, disgusted, a wave of nausea hitting him. His stomach lurched as he spewed vomit everywhere, the acid laced with white eggs. It was too late - he was infected. Grabbing his gun, he lifted it up to his head. The wind howled and danced through the trees, breaking the silence that plagued the Earth.
"They're gone."
Maggots crawled up his leg.
"This is all a dream!" he laughed. "I just have to wake up."
He squeezed the trigger...

Emma Coffey (13)
Lenzie Academy, Lenzie

The Cure That No One Knew Existed

"So this was all a trick?" says Wolski.

Three weeks earlier... The chief was driving and was picking up Wolski to go to the agency. When they arrived, they were greeted by the General. The General gave them their assignment to save the human race. So Wolski and Chief went into the forbidden forest,

"Twelve beasts to kill," Chief said.

As they were going through the forest, they killed half of the twelve. They arrived at the den of the leftover beasts. They burst through the door. There were no beasts, just their general and a gun.

"Sweet home Alabama..."

Evan Hunter (13)
Lenzie Academy, Lenzie

The USA Goes Bananas

Who would've thought bananas could change the world? Every single banana in the USA was infected with a chemical that would make anyone who ate them go crazy. Unfortunately, President Trump had the first poisonous banana and he was deranged. He promoted these bananas so much that almost everyone ate them except a group of girls who were allergic to bananas. Together, the group tried to warn everyone to not eat the bananas, but everyone had already eaten them. They were doomed.

President Trump heard about these girls and was furious. He kidnapped these girls and strangled them to death.

Alvita Tumwijukye (13)
Lenzie Academy, Lenzie

I Shouldn't Have Left

I have been running... for ages! I am going... to run out of breath... really soon. My legs are numb. I shouldn't have left. We were all safe. Not anymore. If I stop, I'll be gone! I will be infected! Everyone has gone insane. Psycho. It's cold and rainy. Winter isn't fun in Scotland, especially while being chased by the 'braindead'! Wow, how am I still running? Oh no, a tree has fallen, blocking the whole road! God, it's really big. I'm going too fast. I have to jump.
"Dammit!"
My head really hurts. I turn around. They're coming...

Kirsty Dunbar (13)
Lenzie Academy, Lenzie

Mission Contamination - Scotland

Time For Humanity To End

John was all alone. He walked through the dark corridors of the building, unable to see anything. The world was destroyed. He didn't know how, but the last thing he had seen was a giant, poisonous-looking cloud coming towards him. Before everything turned upside down. All the adults gone. Or at least, that's what he thought. Missing the past, missing how simple it was, he kept advancing forward. Getting out of this building was his main priority. He heard something behind him. A deep growling noise. Then he saw the glowing of the eyes of a... human... it couldn't be...

Charles Lin (13)
Lenzie Academy, Lenzie

Silence

There had to be a cure somewhere. Dr Phishie paced up and down the lab floor. This parasite had already killed millions. There was barely anyone left alive. 'Silence' would kill everyone and everything that got in its way. The cure was impossible to find. She was scared. Worried her life would be over too soon. *Bang!* The lights went out completely. One of the test chambers exploded open. Two large, decomposing figures crawled over to her. She could tell immediately that they had 'Silence'. Dr Phishie tried to run, but it was too late. Humanity was over.

Abbie McGale (12)
Lenzie Academy, Lenzie

Cruel World

"We live in a cruel world," they say.
I believe them now. I am one of the 4,000 chosen.
"We need to go," I hear them say.
Every year, 4,000 people are chosen for experiments to deal with the world overpopulating.
"Move along."
If we try to run, we get killed instantly.
"Get in and don't try to escape."
We are cramped into a small room. There is nowhere to run. It will all be over soon. Over the next few hours, the room becomes less and less cramped. Until it is only me left. It is time.
Goodbye.

Kayla Ormiston (12)
Lenzie Academy, Lenzie

The Man I Fear Most

The cure had to be here somewhere. I had to fix this broken world. Not many years ago, people started to develop powers. Some quite simple like growing hair quickly, but some incredible like shooting acid from your fingertips. Of course, there's a downside. When you're born, there's a fifty percent chance that this power will corrupt you. You will become a monster. Now, I must find a cure for my family.

In the dead silence, I began to hear the beat of footsteps nearby. Closer, closer, stop. My mindless father now stood before me. Closer, closer, closer...

Lucy Brear (12)
Lenzie Academy, Lenzie

No Hope

We were trapped, stuck in the room designed to protect us from the gas which was infecting the entire population. Now we were all going to die. The room was built to protect us from a physical enemy like the infected people, but when the electricity was taken down, the door automatically locked. The deadly, noxious chemical was seeping through the cracks around the door. If we became infected, we would all turn into the mindless zombie enemy. Desperately, we tried to batter the door off its hinges but it wouldn't budge. Trapped, unable to resist, there was no hope...

Grant Morrison (13)
Lenzie Academy, Lenzie

The Second War

They said it would end the war. All it did was cause a second one. Let's go back to the start where it began. I was clearing out a prison compound of insurgents when they launched a counter-attack. I held them off for as long as I could. Back-up wasn't far away. I heard insurgents grunting through the darkness surrounding me. My ammo was low. I needed back-up.
The head of special forces informed me, "The bomb will be -"
A blast in the distance knocked me down. Soon after, I heard noises. Screaming. The creatures were born. Death came.

Rory Stuart Slorance (14)
Lenzie Academy, Lenzie

Contagion

Population control. Well, that's what it was supposed to be, anyway. We, the government, hired some very intelligent scientists to create a deadly virus that would kill a whole city. Ruthless I know, but it had to be done. It was all going well until someone figured a way out of the massive electric fence we built. Then they infected the whole world.

There was a sudden noise coming from next to me. I looked at everyone. We all knew what was happening. Something outside had opened the bunker door. I could hear deep grunting noises. It was a contagion...

Eva Cameron (13)
Lenzie Academy, Lenzie

The Disease

I was surprised, I was expecting sun but no, everything was dull and bland. As I looked south, I saw a figure that appeared to have its arm hanging off. The outbreak of the disease has been catastrophic on the climate and people. We have been separated from the infected. Because of the disease, rocks have been falling and infecting people. I'm lucky to be alive. The disease is making people turn savage, angry and really pale. It is terrifying that my mum has become infected. I don't know if I will be alive for much longer. Wait... *knock knock!*

Calvin Williamson (13)
Lenzie Academy, Lenzie

The Beetle

As the Huey T7 sped over the barren landscape, the minutes turned to hours. As I looked out the window, something caught my eye. A speck of green gunk was dripping down the window, turning the raindrops to steam. Suddenly, a small dot in the gloop started to grow, turning into a beetle. Now I realised what it was. The beetle that nearly destroyed the country. I panicked.
"We are all going to die!" I screamed.
I was being cornered by the guards. A knock! Then darkness. When I awoke, I felt sick and then something scuttled under my skin...

Angus Lavy (13)
Lenzie Academy, Lenzie

The Break-In

I finally emerged from the underground bunker. It had been a few days since the zombie outbreak started and I didn't get any sleep last night. I didn't know where any of my friends or family were. I was going out to look for them but I would return before dark. I had been watching the news lately and had been noticing that the zombies had been acting stranger and stranger at night. The zombies were outside. I could hear them. There were probably thousands of them. I heard them hitting the door repeatedly. Then *crash!* They had broken in...

Lee Cairns (13)
Lenzie Academy, Lenzie

Acid Cloud

The cloud was replicating, there was acid everywhere, I was the only one alive. I didn't know how much more damage the lab could take. My fate was here and it would not be satisfying. The acid was making a flood like Noah never imagined and it was catastrophic. The lab was shaking mentally and all the chemicals, test tubes and experiments were smashing to bits like priceless artefacts, trying to save them was not necessary as it was too late now. The cloud was replicating more across the continent. There were green chemicals leaking... or was it acid?

Emmanuel Mersha (13)
Lenzie Academy, Lenzie

Gone

Nearly everyone in the town had caught the rash. Giant, poisonous, pus-filled spots blanketed skins throughout the whole town. I was their only hope. I rummaged through the old, dirty test tubes and looked under the files of past scientists. Nothing. I knew the antidote was somewhere in here so I looked around for possible places. The walls in this lab were covered in slime and gunge, not to mention the stains on the roof. Something scuttled under my skin. The rash was spreading, pulsing, hurting. I knew I was their last hope, but it had gotten me too...

Eva Coleman (12)
Lenzie Academy, Lenzie

Trying For Survival

Months had passed. How long could a disease go on for? Running out of food and water, what choice did they have? Lucy knew that going out was their only hope, but Marco didn't want to face the consequences. He loved his little sister too much and no one knew how it spread, how to avoid it. Air, water - could be anything. Before trusted scientists got around to investigating it, it had murdered half the population. The time had come. What was worse? Starvation or fatal disease? Opening the heavy doors, Lucy had to try. One last chance at survival...

Rebecca Griffiths (13)
Lenzie Academy, Lenzie

Dome

As I wake up from the empty, dark dome, I feel like I never slept at all because all I hear is the annoying zombies, groaning and banging their heads against the thick glass. I'm worried if I'll ever survive in here. My food supplies are nearly gone so I'll have to go out and get some more before I starve to death. I feel so bored and lonely.
Bang! Bang! Bang! This catches my attention. Is this the zombies finally going to break in? *Kaboom!* Shattered glass raining all around, sending me back into the dark oblivion...

Steven Murphy (13)
Lenzie Academy, Lenzie

The Lab Of Disaster

The rash was spreading, pulsing, hurting. Blood was gushing out of my arm. Whilst sweating heavily, I pulled myself up using a metal desk. My legs were weak. I grabbed a scruffy bandage off the desk and wrapped it around my arm. The zombie was fast and nimble. I didn't expect it. A disinfectant had to be here somewhere. Without it, I would become one of them. Scanning the desk, I searched for it. There it was. *Growl!* I turned around immediately. A zombie was sprinting towards me. I jumped for the needle. My arm extended, as did its own...

Sam Street (14)
Lenzie Academy, Lenzie

The Mystery Of The Creatures

Dear Diary,

Yesterday was a very terrifying night. No one could save her from her horrifying fate. The mysterious creatures were biting, scratching, crawling into her skin and she knew she wasn't going to be able to escape. All of a sudden, they vanished into thin air. As she was coughing up blood, she wondered where they disappeared to. I knew she was very badly contaminated from the creatures and I knew she was going to die from this deadly disease. I had a strong feeling there was a cure somewhere. But it was too late. Her time was up...

Safa Hady (13)
Lenzie Academy, Lenzie

Hairy Havoc

"Test subject A is unaccounted for," said the doctor.
Youngest Drilla and himself had found the virus that had turned everyone but them into werewolves. It was a high-contagious virus if you were touched once. They knew there was no cure. They had tried. They needed to go to Mars.
They could see the space centre. The doctor tripped and the deranged werewolves swarmed and ate him. Drilla ran and got to the rocket and got inside the rocket for Mars. The rocket shot away. Drilla was never seen again and the werewolves ruled Earth.

Angus John Davie (13)
Lenzie Academy, Lenzie

A Tree-Free World

I entered the top security science lab to observe my recent project. My eyes lit up as I spotted my untouched experient. Lifting it up to view my creation further, I noticed leaves. Branches. A trunk. My tree was shockingly coming along extremely well. As excited as a child at Christmas, I raised up my origination and sauntered out of the room. Suddenly, an infectious bug crawled out of my sleeve, tickling my hand. I yelped and, to my horror, dropped my thriving tree. I collapsed to the ground in tears. Is there no hope for our tree-free world?

Hannah Campbell (12)
Lenzie Academy, Lenzie

The Deadly Water

We finally emerged from the underground bunker. Two months passed and we started to run out of food, but we were all scared of what was outside. The last thing that we heard about the virus was that it was spread through contaminated water which made every water source deadly. We managed to survive drinking bottled water that was in the bunker before the water went bad. It was hard to keep going because we kept on finding people trying to survive. But last week, someone broke into the bunker during the night and stole half of the water supply.

Ryan Murray (12)
Lenzie Academy, Lenzie

Fight For Survival

The giant, poisonous cloud rose into the sky of Syria where thousands of people were at war. An eerie atmosphere surrounded everyone and diseases were spreading. People were dropping like flies by the cause of the viruses and one disease could spread all over the globe. There was only one way to survive - by going to a different planet, but it was a slim chance you'd get out alive. Nearly the whole globe had been infected and there was only one man left and his name was Albert Frankenstein. He was surrounded, but he knew he had to try.

Cameron McIntyre (13)
Lenzie Academy, Lenzie

The Bug

A disease is plaguing the world. A bug. A lethal, terrifying, disgusting bug with legs as sharp as needles and see-through skin. I will never forget the day I saw one. The purple liquid flowing through it terrified me, its dagger-like teeth bared. That's how it kills so many people. It latches onto your arm and burrows its way under your skin, then it injects the purple liquid. It makes you crazy. Finally, it eats away at your brain until nothing is left. That's when I feel it; something is under my skin scuttling up to my brain...

Erica Wright (12)
Lenzie Academy, Lenzie

Get Me Out Of Here!

With a dull, gloomy look, it looks like the world is turning into some type of dungeon. I can see the cloud gradually getting larger with a small tint of lime green. A small drop of lime green, yellow liquid drops down towards me, as if it is a bullet firing at me. Slowly, the earth starts to disappear. What is happening? Everything is gone, am I disappearing? My flesh is drifting and flaking away. I can't see anything. It's burning my eyes. The cloud feels like it's taking over the world. This is doom! Get me out of here!

Rhia Lotay (12)
Lenzie Academy, Lenzie

The Bunker Hidden Underground

A boy came out of an underground bunker. There were no living things outside. No trees or plants. Nothing. As he took a breath, he felt his lungs fill with unexplainable air. He hauled his legs over the lump on the ground that was once a beautiful, luscious flower. The ground didn't feel safe. He felt the earth sink beneath his feet. A few minutes later, he looked down. One of his feet had gone! It had sunk into the ground! That's when he realised... the ground was not the ground at all, but was a pit of contaminated liquids.

Victoria Elena Wilson (12)
Lenzie Academy, Lenzie

Human Contact

It had been months. Months since any human contact. I knew that one day I would run out of food and water, but I didn't expect it to be so soon. I nervously slammed open the heavy door and looked around. There was nothing but dead bodies. The city of Glasgow was ruined. *Stay focused*, I thought to myself as I hopped into an almost-destroyed car and sped over to the hospital. I knew the cure had to be here somewhere. I rifled through the messy cabinets until, suddenly, I heard something. *Crack!* I was not alone...

Molly Rush (12)
Lenzie Academy, Lenzie

The Last Video

"I am Dr Drencht and if you are watching this video, you need to hurry up. Me and my helper, Mr Fletour, found a virus named TAY. You need to be careful. There is one left: the most dangerous. To kill him, put water on his body. You are our only chance to save the Earth and one last thing, never look at his... arghhhhh! No! They got the doctor! I need to kill this virus."
But when I looked outside, the contamination was spreading, hurting... I needed to be quick. *Boom!* He was here with everyone. I was alone.

Angelina Vignal (12)
Lenzie Academy, Lenzie

The Scientists Of Iceland

The rash was spreading and pulsing, hurting billions of people around the globe. But only one country had survived: Iceland! Hólmavík was the last town alive. But the lucky scientists who lived in a cave in the mountains were the last to survive. It was their mission to save themselves and the rest of the population. When the last drop of the liquid for the cure fell into the test tube, they could finally emerge from the mountains to inject the cure into all the ill people. This would make the world a better place.

Greg Duncan (13)
Lenzie Academy, Lenzie

Restart My World

Here it comes. Louder, faster, angrier, heading for me! I have a feeling it's not going to kill me... It's just going to hurt me. Really... really... bad. I just need to run and run fast. I've been moving about for days. This disgusting disease, this illness, this parasite, it will end the world. I need to find somewhere safe for me. I need to dash through my hometown to at least try to get away. If the monster is not going down easily, then neither am I. Not without a fight, anyway. I'm going to try and make it.

Stewart Forrest (14)
Lenzie Academy, Lenzie

Contraband

How will this end? Dr Kay has been studying Contraband for years. Contraband was originally found in dogs. It spreads by contact and claims the mind quickly. A dark figure looms over Dr Kay and grabs her hand. She shrieks and tries to run, but this figure is strong. He's trying to pass on Contraband. She finally breaks free but it's too late. The distinct mark of Contraband is visible on her wrist. The rash is spreading, pulsing, hurting... This is the end for Dr Kay. But it is just the beginning for Contraband...

Erin Leia Galloway (13)
Lenzie Academy, Lenzie

The Cure

Hunter's army are killers. We're living in fear of our own people. The people here are dying day in, day out. At the start, there were twenty of us, now there are only five, trying to get rid of the disease. Hunter and his army are turning innocent people into murderous monsters. We are trying to find cures. A way to stop this. We who are not infected are constantly trying to get to the end of this day and night. Everyone who had not been killed or infected by the disease is playing a game. A game called life...

Bethyn Lyall (12)
Lenzie Academy, Lenzie

The End

Dark. dull. It looked like the whole world had been ripped up by a bright, burning fire. They let us out, but I didn't dare to walk out into the black, ashy world first. Trying to hold back. Failing, the horde of people just kept walking through. Eventually, I had to walk out into the alien-like world. Just as I was about to step outside, I saw someone from school. Then I saw panic on everyone's faces. I turned left. What looked like a ball of fire was racing towards us. I knew these would be my last moments...

Ewan O'Hara (13)
Lenzie Academy, Lenzie

The Cure

As I walked into the lab, I could not believe my eyes. Ripping! Shredding! Screeching! Everyone's life in pieces. I could see the robots, shiny and clean, obeying their true master. Then they released a poisonous gas into the air.

The cure had to be here somewhere. I couldn't find it so I converted zinc with iron and put sulfate to make a *boom!* All the robots had broken into bits and pieces. After this, I broke into the lab so I could find the cure. I saw so many test tubes. But which one was it?

Aisha Ali (13)
Lenzie Academy, Lenzie

The Ligma

We finally emerged from the underground bunker. The Light was spreading. All the contaminated zombies with ligma stared right into my eyes. I already had stage one ligma, which was okay, but if I got stage three, I would turn into a zombie! I grabbed my gun, I thought I would loot some zombies. Then I put on my protective gear. "Yes!" I screamed.

It had bullets in its pockets, five to be precise. So I decided to return to the bunker. All my friends had a party because of the wonderful bullets.

Hamish Grant Robertson (12)
Lenzie Academy, Lenzie

The Bright Sky

The giant, poisonous cloud rose into the sky... why would God do this? I tried to think about the good times I had with my family before they were taken away by those things. I saw an underground bunker and ran to safety. The smell inside was revolting. There were a lot of rotting corpses as I went deeper into the old bunker. The bunker shook as the bomb hit the town. I hid under a table and waited for it to stop. *Bang!* A loud explosion came from the room next to me, then I realised I wasn't alone...

Connor McKinnon (13)
Lenzie Academy, Lenzie

1, 2, 3... How Many More?

The cure had to be somewhere. My best friend, Alana, and I were trapped in the dark woods with the small but fierce wolf children. We rushed to the top of a tall tree, thinking we were safe, but to our surprise, they were able to climb! My heart was pounding fast, my face was as pale as snow. I had no choice other than to jump off. I lay on the ground. *Crunch!* I called out for Alana. There was no response. I realised that my best friend, the person I could depend on, was contaminated. I was alone...

Maryam Mian (12)
Lenzie Academy, Lenzie

The Allergy

Today has been the worst day ever, it started off really well. I liked George. He was tall with blonde hair. I told him about my allergy to rain but he didn't mind. We were sitting in my room until George had to leave. I walked him to the door. He ran outside because it was pouring with rain. All of a sudden, he dropped to the ground. I was confused. He was just lying in the middle of the road. Cars stopped to see what had happened. Then it clicked - George had my allergy. I think it's contagious...

Rebecca Howie (13)
Lenzie Academy, Lenzie

Run

We finally emerged from the underground bunker. The light hit my face, blinding me. The feeling of what could be waiting for us burnt me almost as much as the dark red sun that seemed to engulf the sky. So off we set out, back to the place we used to call home. As we walked, I heard a faint rumble, then darkness. There it was, as tall as tall could be. It blocked out the sun with its finger. Its eye was like a spotlight, a beam staring down at us, blinding us. We couldn't do anything but run...

Adam Farrel (12)
Lenzie Academy, Lenzie

Mushroom

The giant, poisonous cloud rose into the sky. A mushroom bomb filled with itching powder, the wind brought it closer and closer. People screaming. I felt helpless. I was a scientist and we were making spacesuits. I was testing the water resistance when it fell. This war with Russia was getting out of hand. I decided to return to work. It had been three days since the bomb fell. I cracked the antidote, we started to mass produce it then I realised that I did not write down the recipe.

Oliver Leo Barrie (12)
Lenzie Academy, Lenzie

Contaminated Airport

As I took a step onto the plane, everyone was dead with bites taken out of them. I saw some creatures at the back. They ran towards me, then I jumped back out the plane and slammed the door. The whole airport was empty. Running around, I looked for someone, then the whole building started shaking. I fell down and was hurt because, after I fell, I was shaken around and all of the building was falling apart. A creature appeared and ran towards me. I sprinted away and started to scream.

Ross Cunningham (13)
Lenzie Academy, Lenzie

What's Above...?

We finally emerged from the underground bunker. It was so bright, it felt like I was going blind. I finally came back to normal, but as my eyes focused, my mum fell to the ground. This creature I had never seen before, it was right behind my mum. I looked down, my mum had big red spots on her whole body. Now there were more of the creatures near us. It was like a human turned into a zombie but with teeth like a shark. They were all coming towards us now, then I knew it was the end.

Kayleigh McKeown (12)
Lenzie Academy, Lenzie

Test Subject D

The computers hummed as Test Subject B came into the test zone. I had to hurry, I was the one who had to figure out how to kill them. I aimed the weapon and fired. Nothing happened. The same with Subject C, but it was Subject D that did it. The flames shot out, the creature turned to flames and the protective glass burst. No power, no light, no way out. I was done for. The monster crashed through, grabbing all the weapons. They weren't as dumb as they looked.

Cameron Borthwick (12)
Lenzie Academy, Lenzie

Weapon S

"Top secret operation Weapon S has gone horribly wrong."
"We can't locate Saber or Death subjects but they're still in here, send help..."
"Arghhhhh!"
The entire lab was filled with corpses, ripped in half and limbs missing. The mutants burst out, went on a murderous rampage, ripping up all in their path. The military arrived.
"There!"
The men blew the mass of bone and muscles' head off, bits everywhere but it grew back. The red-furred one ripped two in half. The big one released a spore and infected them, transforming like him. Will anyone survive?

Campbell Robertson (12)
Speyside High School, Aberlour

Science Lab

"What happened? What went wrong?" someone said in horror.

"Don't panic, we just need to stop it before it spreads!"

"Oh no, it's too late."

Before they could stop it, it had spread around the whole school. Who was to blame? The whole school had been infected. No one could save them. But how were they infected? It all started with Jessica in the science lab with Mr White. They were doing an experiment. It went wrong and it spread into the canteen and got into the food. Everyone there ate the food and were poisoned then they all died.

Emma Nicoll (12)
Speyside High School, Aberlour

The Purple Monsters

The last drop fell into the test tube. Professor Spoon had just finished planning his new and improved babies experiment. He started to walk towards the door when suddenly, *boom!* The glass tubes smashed all over the floor. Screams were heading out the door and soon all over the cities. They were hairy, purple little creatures with blue hair and orange bumps all over their slimy skin. They ran round the city, causing chaos. They quickly worked their way around the city from schools to parks, terrorising everyone. Everyone was searching for a cure. It had to be somewhere...

Molly Bailey (12)
Speyside High School, Aberlour

Contaminated

The last drop fell into the test tube, but in mid-air, the bubble popped and went all over the teacher. After a few seconds, the teacher had disappeared. I thought to myself, *what on Earth? How could that have happened? What had those pupils been doing?* I went into the back room and there was a cleaning product called 'Vanish'. Before I knew it, all the teachers had disappeared. I picked up the bottle and it said *Makes things disappear.* To get them back, it says, *Shout "Vanish, come back!"* I called it and it worked. Mission complete!

Chelsea Hewitt (13)
Speyside High School, Aberlour

The Murderous Sweetie

The last member of the Swizzles family is bored of the company so he hands it on to this so-called 'sweetie expert'. He makes some changes to the sweetie, thinking it would taste better, but little did he know it was a recipe for disaster!

Every consumer that had eaten the Fizzers had forgotten everything and had the desire to murder everyone. The whole population was doomed and no one knew why.

As well as the desire to kill and memory loss, people were coughing up blood.

Even the 'sweetie expert' died and the only life left was animals!

Lucy Grant (13)
Speyside High School, Aberlour

Apocalypse

Bang! I looked at my mother. Her blood-drizzled face turned white, her hazel eyes wide with fear. My little sister squeezed what was left of her muddy teddy, her clothes ripped to shreds, showing her bruised skin, her face covered by her brown hair. I turned to my father. He had a sharp, broken stick.
"Grab something! Anything!" he said, lip bleeding, eyes full of fear.
Everyone hurried. I found an old mop, turned to the door. It burst open. My heart thumping, I fell forwards, my face blank, eyes glued shut as I greeted a brutal death...

Jasmine Mears (13)
Speyside High School, Aberlour

The Demon

In the hidden lab in the research facility, a scientist was tampering with the DNA of a man who had lost his family to a strange disease. He had nothing left to lose. The modifications had caused him to lose control and become a horrifying demon. The scientist screamed as the once human man's spine tore through his back, blood spilling everywhere. The lights went out and the demon let out a disgusting screech before running to the scientist, tearing him in half. Humanity was almost gone, there were dead bodies and limbs everywhere. The demon was outside now.

Luca Iannetta (12)
Speyside High School, Aberlour

Operation Outbreak

I emerged from my bunker, only knowing I needed to find a cure for the entire town. I was trying to stay hidden from the brainless, mutants but it didn't work. They recognised me. Well, I didn't exactly blend in...

I finally reached the lab. I saw a list of ingredients for the cure. I scavenged the lab while fighting off the infected. I made the cure. I thought the windmill could spread the cure but realised that I had been infected. I got hit. I headed to the windmill. I turned it on, the cure spread. "Operation Outbreak succeeds."

Connor Spence (13)
Speyside High School, Aberlour

It's The End...

Infections are spreading around the city, killing people every day. There is nowhere to run, nowhere to hide. All humans will die due to hunger, the disease or both. The world is coming to an end, animals dying, plants dying, humans dying, but most importantly, the dome shielding the city is cracking. Days pass, the Earth is getting worse. The dome has cracked. There are about ten humans remaining. The infection is all over the city. The remaining humans have no choice but to go outside and accept their deaths. The humans lined up and then they all died sadly.

Mackenzie Duthie (12)
Speyside High School, Aberlour

The Symbiote

One late night, Eddie, who is a reporter, gets a call and is told to go to a lab called 'Life'. He looks at different people within the lab and Eddie is shocked at what he is seeing, as he witnesses many people with weird side effects whilst they are being tested.

Then suddenly... a lady is banging her hands, screaming, "Get me out!" Eddie grabs a fire extinguisher and bashes it against the glass, breaking it and then enters and is contaminated with what she has. It's called Symbiote. He can hear voices, but... are they good or bad?

Ethan Thomson (13)
Speyside High School, Aberlour

Mixture Menace

Professor Callahan was working on a new experiment to save people from all types of cancer. He accidentally slipped and coated the mixture on himself. Suddenly, he grew large scales, larger spikes began to grow on his back. The man's vision changed, he didn't know who he was at all. All he knew and all he thought was to touch people to infect them with his germs. Suddenly, he broke free of the lab and began to infect everyone that crossed his path. Soon, almost the whole world was infected by his bug. However, their existence now lived in space.

Nancy Sunshine Stewart (12)
Speyside High School, Aberlour

Intense Infection

There is an infection going around every person. Sometimes, I think these scientists here in the UK are actually trying to kill us. I mean, who mixes medicines that can wipe out the whole human race? The experiments usually work. They didn't this time. We have to grab our things and hide. The weak will die first. Then eventually, the strong will give up. Nothing can beat this. The only solution is to start hiding in the ground. All the weak are dying. There are piles of them stacked up everywhere you look. It could be anyone next. Maybe me...

Aimee Anne Hay (12)
Speyside High School, Aberlour

Injections

The NHS sent out injections to everyone, unaware of the dangerous toxins in them. The shot was to prevent cancer, which it did, but also had a killing bacteria in it. Everyone who got the shot would be dead in about ten days. It was all over the news but it was too late. Everyone in the world would die. Even if they hadn't gotten the injections, it was highly contagious from sneezing, coughing and breathing. It started spreading from Scotland and was travelling very fast. There would be no future for anyone unless we could find a cure, fast.

Alexis Stuart (13)
Speyside High School, Aberlour

Bacteria

Happening in a retro-futuristic 1960, there is an infectious bacteria swarming about Earth. If you get infected, you will melt where you stand. In two days, it needs to be eradicated or else the human race is at stake. Four medics need to figure out a cure to the bacteria or they're going to die as well. The wind blowing a gale, pushing the bacteria into every nook and cranny, eventually making it into the bunker before they could make the cure, killing all of them except one who got to a vacuum chamber in time. Days later, they're dead.

Jake Urquhart (13)
Speyside High School, Aberlour

Evacuation

The year is 2054, the Earth is overrun by mutant insects and the human population was down to the mere number of 50,000. It all started when there was a new insect killer, but instead of killing them, it acted like steroids enlarging them. There was one final plan to restore the Earth to its past glory: a bomb of lethal insect killer. People were ordered to take shelter in an enormous army bunker. Every remaining human being did as they were ordered, quickly. When the bomb hit, everyone was safe, the mission was a success. Mission accomplished.

Edward Kendrick (13)
Speyside High School, Aberlour

The Deadly Spillage

The lorry crashed, spilling gas, brains and dead corpses. The magnetic ray pulled everyone and they turned into brain-thirsty zombies.The zombies chased me. I ran into the science lab, throwing bottles everywhere. They smashed. I heard the zombies on the door. I screamed. It was like the glass was going to smash. There was blood everywhere. The zombies had bitten off their arms. The blood touched me.
I screamed, "There must be a cure somewhere!" Yellow boils and burns covered my skin, popping! I couldn't see a thing.

Olivia Mitchell (12)
Speyside High School, Aberlour

Aiden And The Contaminated Centre

Aiden woke up and all he saw above him were dead corpses with blood pods leaking out their eyes, ears and mouths. Then he stood up and looked around him. He saw he was surrounded by corpses, then he saw normal people were past a glass wall. Aiden then realised he was in a containment centre. These things looked like Gollum and looked like they were trying to break out but didn't move. Then, suddenly, they chased and attacked Aiden! The next thing Aiden saw was a pool of blood and bleeding guts leaking out his side before pitch-black...

Thomas Neil Gordon Stepien (12)
Speyside High School, Aberlour

Infected

The last drop fell into the test tube. Bob was so excited that his new make-up formula was complete.
"Can I try it?" I asked,
"Of course," Bob said.
I put the make-up onto my face. It started bulging out. Bubbling! Bursting! These massive boils started forming on my face. I didn't know what to do. They started squirting out this black substance. It got on Bob. He screamed as he tried to get away. Soon, it was on everyone. Everyone was infected. These massive boils were on everyone. Would we survive?

Martha Morton (12)
Speyside High School, Aberlour

A Creature In The Dark

Something was out there but he didn't know what. He walked through the alleyways in fear, then he heard a twig crack. He swooped round. "Arghhhhh!" The sound was blood-curdling.

The next morning, he woke up lying down in the alleyway. There was a huge bite mark on his shoulder, it was gushing with blood. A rash was starting to form, turning a greeny-brown colour and his skin was peeling badly. He stood up and realised it was worse than he thought. The rash soared down his leg. It was spreading, pulsing, hurting...

Katie Jean Walker (12)
Speyside High School, Aberlour

Gas In The Air!

The giant cloud rose into the sky. North Korea just fired a nuke into the middle of Russia and many people were dying because the gas was going through the air. They built a massive bunker to survive and got resources such as food, water, medicines and clothes. Many people travelled to the bunker to seek refuge. When they got in, they just had enough supplies but they sadly watched people outside die. They got out after the wind blew the gas away, the people in the bunker survived and went back to their country and home and were happy.

Josh Shaw-Rose (13)
Speyside High School, Aberlour

Midge Ghost

Midges are coming down from the sky like rain. They will sink into your skin. Once they are in your skin, they will multiply. The midges will eat all your organs and your veins, then you will turn into a ghost. A scientist is making medication to kill the midges. People are hiding so they don't get the midges but they go everywhere. The whole world is infected with midges' ghosts. The scientist is just finishing with the medication and it is in a humongous cylinder. He put it into the ghost humans to fix them. Will it work?

Luke Mackie (13)
Speyside High School, Aberlour

The Train

He pulled off his jumper. Four hours still to go. I could see massive yellow bubbles on his arms. I'd never seen anything like it. Then, the massive bubble burst. The pus went everywhere. Then another one burst. I tried to shuffle away but it was too late. Everyone was turning into monsters. The train stopped. I could see the driver fall to the floor. We were trapped. All I could see was the monster's eyes glaring at me. They slapped the window as the emergency light flickered. I paused, thinking how I was going to escape.

Leah Wendy McGillivray (12)
Speyside High School, Aberlour

Digest Disaster

It was a normal Monday afternoon. Nobody knew within twenty-four hours the whole country would be shut down. It was eleven at night. I was carting the digest from McPherson's van. An idiot pulled out in front of me. I swerved to avoid the car but I went into a lake and all the digest went into it. It was a code-red situation. Within half an hour, the disease had spread fifty miles. Now, the country couldn't import food. It was five weeks before the problem was fixed. As for the drivers of the car, they were sent to jail.

Ian Forsyth (13)
Speyside High School, Aberlour

Them...

This world is horrible. They bang on the doors, constantly screaming. I can't sleep. There are people that turn, turn into these spindly, tall entities. When this disease starts to affect people, they tear the limbs off of you, it's horrible... How they kill is to tear your limbs off, they grab your jaw and rip it away from your skull. You can feel every second of that torture... And that was the last thing I felt before I exhaled one last time. If only I was lucky enough to become one of them with a simple bite...

Jamie Boyd (12)
Speyside High School, Aberlour

It Continues

Cure A had stopped infections for years. It stopped us from turning or feeling like a zombie. Everyone who didn't take it was dead. They were all dead. More people took this medicine over the years and had no worries... but we were wrong. We had to destroy this medicine as fast as we could. Children, babies, parents and the elderly were taking this and it had to stop. We didn't know this was going to happen. We never expected it. We had to find another cure to stop this and fast. We all knew we were going to die.

Jessica Knox (12)
Speyside High School, Aberlour

Bloodsuckers

The bug-like shape was crawling up my arm, slowly making its way towards my neck. The same thing happened to my brother and my dad. Now they are in intensive care, fighting for their lives. The bug is growing, feeding on my blood. My mum won't let me in the house. I'm getting cold, my skin is turning pale. The scientists said on the news that an experiment went horribly wrong and billions of these bug-like creatures have escaped. They said that the bugs feed on human blood. How much longer will I be alive for?

Catriona Lily Bothwell (12)
Speyside High School, Aberlour

The Walking City Of The Dead

The infection had nearly taken everybody in the city. The zombies were everywhere. I was having to hide in my underground bunker, it was dark and gloomy. I finally decided to emerge from my bunker. I took one look. I saw a walking city of the dead. I needed to get out of this city. There was nothing around. I legged it. I glanced behind. A huge, yellow-eyed creature with guts and blood coming out of his oversized mouth growled at me. I screamed so loud, windows cracked. It bit me. A spreading rash formed. Help!

Jack McConnachie (13)
Speyside High School, Aberlour

Wipe Out!

"Drive!"

The zombies were surrounding them now. They had to escape. Fred stepped on it, they had to get the cure. The only problem was the lab was surrounded by a wall. They approached the wall. They managed to sneak into a bit where the wall was damaged but there were no people around and all of a sudden, a glimpse of the zombies. They ran but Shaggy fell over and was bitten. He then caught up with Scooby, he ate him and Scooby burst out of his stomach. They then ate the rest of them. Wipe out!

Archie Bain (12)
Speyside High School, Aberlour

No One Would Survive…

The rash was spreading, pulsing, hurting. A scientist spilt chemicals in the air. Mosquitoes inhaled the air and all of them became poisonous. I was walking and one bit me. That was how I got the rash. It poisoned the plants and water too. No one could drink or eat. Many people were dead around me. Stacks of bodies for miles and miles. I fell down, gasping for air. The rash had spread up to my throat. I could not move. Now no one could help me. Everyone I could see was dead. I was in agony. None would survive.

Abbie Ettles (12)
Speyside High School, Aberlour

The Disease Killing Everyone

We finally emerged from the underground bunker. There was a gas explosion and people were turning green, crispy and had no heads. They would eat you with their mouth and were so fast you couldn't run. One day, I saw one walk into a school and eat everyone and then spat them out as one of them. I heard the kids screaming and shouting. They started to form eyes on their chest and ears on their arms. There was a yellow one and it was three times faster and ate 100 people in ten seconds. Now everyone was gone.

Matthew McConachie (12)
Speyside High School, Aberlour

Contaminated School Corridors

One winter morning, these kids at school were walking in the corridors of St. Nicolas Primary School. They were all nervous because they thought they were going to be killed and they did not want to go to school ever again. The next day, they had to go to school but luckily, the school was not contaminated anymore so the kids were sad. School was open again. Their teacher was not at school so they had to get the teacher they hated so much. The teacher was so happy to teach them. But the kids were not...

Keirenza Catriona Garden (13)
Speyside High School, Aberlour

The Lab Incident

It was just an experiment at the start but something happened. We were told that one of the corpses was gone and two guards went missing and then we found them. They were undead. In just an hour, everyone was infected. The lab was put on lockdown. I saw them trying to break down the bulletproof door and now, I am the only survivor. I am running out of food and I only have two bullets left and if you are reading this: shoot their heads! Hold on, they just broke down the door... great. This is my end.

Millan Ormsby (14)
Speyside High School, Aberlour

Night Out With Friends

Night out with friends, we were at Aberlar Bars. Before I walked in, I saw a purple cloud. I ran back home. I was watching from my window and saw everyone drop to the ground. Then they got back up, they looked like zombies. I had to act fast or they would get into my house, so I grabbed old wood from the garage and boarded up my windows. I ran back upstairs and found a book about how to get zombies away. I tried it and it worked. The secret potion worked. I'm lucky that was in the book.

Myles Hardie (12)
Speyside High School, Aberlour

Infected

The giant mushroom cloud rose into the sky. I was scared. I ran into the bunker. Two days later, *bang! Bang! Bang!* I had heard the infected banging on the door for two days straight. Suddenly, the banging stopped. I thought I might check if there was anybody around, I opened the bunker door. I stepped out. I could see a horde in the distance, they were infected. My arm was red and puffy, it felt like it was about to burst. I lay down and waited, I was infected. Was I going to die?

Ben Charleworth (12)
Speyside High School, Aberlour

Zombie Apocalypse

We had been stuck down here for days. We had very little food and drink. We had to send someone out to get supplies but that was very risky as they might inhale, turning them into a zombie like the rest of the city. We had to get food and water so we sent a group off.

Many hours later, we heard a grumble coming from outside. They seemed to be getting louder and louder. Then we heard a knock on the hatch. We opened it up and find a horde of gruesome, armless zombies hungry for flesh.

Archie Scott (12)
Speyside High School, Aberlour

The Infection

The infection: poisonous, deadly and spreading fast, I wouldn't last here for long. No food, no water, I would starve. I had to get out of here, it was impossible to stay alive down here. I eventually found a way out but I was cautious to leave. I had to survive one way. I opened the large steel door, the clouds were grey and it was dark and nothing was in sight. I was surrounded by the disease, I was cold. I could die out here. There's no way I would live... Not out here anyway.

Sarah Robertson (12)
Speyside High School, Aberlour

Was He A Science Teacher?

As the last drop fell into the test tube, the science teacher was happy for us to use these new chemicals, but he seemed a bit too happy. He had told us about these new chemicals for weeks and when putting that last drop into the test tube, all he did was smile. He told us more instructions, what to put into the test tube, but nothing happened... then the coughing appeared, then gigantic lumps all over our faces which were oozing yellow sap. Then, all of a sudden, we had no heartbeat.

Keisha McGill (12)
Speyside High School, Aberlour

Deep Holes

I finally emerged from the underground bunker away from the bloodsucking leeches. I had big black holes in my arms and legs. They were leaking everywhere. I came to a halt to see if they were following me. The holes were hurting. They ached. I felt weak and tired. You could see the bone. All of a sudden, I heard a squelching sound. I didn't dare look. I just ran. I suddenly ran out of breath. They were gaining on me. They caught up with me. They sucked all my blood so I died.

Amanda Watson (12)
Speyside High School, Aberlour

Welcome To The Russian Wasteland

We were watching TV on Sunday. There was a knock on the door. I got it. There was a sign saying: *WWIII by the Russian men.* So I told my dad. He told us to go down into the bunker so we were safe. There were footsteps above us. It was the Russians spreading toxic waste around us. Therefore, we kept super silent. Then they went away. We heard a jeep outside so we went to see and it was one of ours with all the stuff we needed so we got out of there after all.

Cailean Dyer (13)
Speyside High School, Aberlour

Zombie Outbreak

Something scuttled under my skin, I felt it running around, nibbling at my skin. I'm not sure how a mini creature like this could get into my skin. A few days ago, an old man came up to me and bit me. Ever since then, I haven't felt right. My skin has turned very pale and all over my body there are big, red, itchy boils. They pop every time I scratch them. Yesterday, I bit someone on the street. I think I might be turning into one of them...

Macy Catherine Furness (13)
Speyside High School, Aberlour

A Thing On My Skin

The rash was spreading, pulsing, hurting. I had no clue what it was. I was sweating and felt very tired and unwell. My room was in the basement. I tried to get up from my bed. I tried to use my phone but I couldn't even put the password in and the Wi-Fi was strangely off. I couldn't even hear cars and lorries going by my house. I looked down at my arm and the thing on my arm was spreading to my legs and chest. What was this infection?

Ethan McIntosh (12)
Speyside High School, Aberlour

Test Subject 101

Something scuttled under my skin. I twitched, tracing the virus' mosaic motif down my forearm. Being selected to test the antidote many considered a gift. The chance to live, breathe and survive another day... But I knew, with ever-increasing mortality rates, I stood about as much chance of survival as the last test subjects. The crawling up my spine curled into a fist, clutching, twisting, hurting... *click!* The door swung open, presenting a scientist, clad in white, brandishing a blood-red syringe. My stomach lurched.
"It's your lucky day!" he brawled, looming closer. Eyes squeezed shut, pain's epitome enveloped me.

Sophie Rachael Reid (16)
St George's School For Girls, Edinburgh

Slaves

"Move!"

The guard jammed the muzzle of his rifle into the back of the girl's head.

"Testing time..."

"No!"

The girl spun around and before he could do anything, threw a lightning-fast punch at his face, shattering his nose. These people wanted to create mindless slaves by injecting people with a drug that would take their free will. It wasn't working though. They had killed many in the process, but Emily was determined not to share that same fate.

"The test subject has escaped!"

Time was running out. Someone had set off the alarms. Emily needed to escape. Now!

Molly Mathers (11)
St George's School For Girls, Edinburgh

The Last Survivors

We finally emerged from the underground bunker. Light covered the Earth like a blanket, filling it with warmth and comfort. Comfort - something we hadn't had for twenty years. We scanned the uninhabited land, hoping, praying for more survivors. But there were none, all we were left with were the remains of our people displayed across the ground for us to see. How would we survive? The remaining looked towards the horizon and in the distance, the trees whispered as if calling to us, compelling us into the unknown. Taking tentative steps, overwhelming dread suffocated. There was no life here...

Niranjana Gopalakrishnan (16)
St George's School For Girls, Edinburgh

Where Am I?

Bleep! Bleep! A small circle of white light comes into view. *Bleep! Bleep!* The light is growling and multiplying. Suddenly, my head starts throbbing again, but not like before it feels like my eyes are bursting out of my skull! The dots are growing into lines and the lines are forming letters that are floating up in front of me towards the... wait, where's the roof? Where are the walls? Where am I? Standing, I get a better view of the black void surrounding me. Sounds of keys being pressed echo as the letters become words: 'Welcome to the virus.'

Heidi Masters (12)
St George's School For Girls, Edinburgh

Promise Me

"Close your eyes. Tight. Really tight, so that you can't see anything. Hold your breath. Hold it as long as you can. The second you open it, it could all be over. All of it, everything, so don't. Promise me, now! You won't breathe or open it? You won't understand now, but you will. What's in there could destroy you."
I told him that but of course, young boys don't always listen to their fathers, they are curious and playful. That is their one fault. Because he opened it, he is dead and I am running from whatever it is.

Amber Devin (15)
St George's School For Girls, Edinburgh

Blackout

She jumped into the water. It felt different, it felt colder than before and it was pricking her neck. After a while, she passed a sign, it read *Beware: Chemicals*. She started to cough and splutter and then she blacked out. Everything was blurred and she could hear the rattling of wheels. She was on a hospital bed, she could see many blue dots crowding round her and there were worried voices echoing around the room but the noise that was the loudest was the mobile. *Beep beep!* All of a sudden, her heart slowed down, the monitor stopped.

Jemima Macaulay (11)
St George's School For Girls, Edinburgh

One Touch

"There he is!" I shouted at the professors who were frantically mixing test tubes together.

I sprinted towards my dying husband. As I got closer I could see the infectious disease taking over him. His feet, then ankles, then his legs were turning a chilling blue colour until he could not feel them anymore. I knelt beside him, wiping my tears away.

I could just make out his last words before he died, "I love you, but don't come near me otherwise you will die too..."

The urge was too strong, I knelt and kissed him.

Evie McCallum
St George's School For Girls, Edinburgh

How Could This Happen?

A giant, poisonous cloud rises into the sky... how could this happen? I have only been gone for a week. My grandfather's Russian bomb exploded, causing a nuclear reaction which formed an ominous cloud. Oh no! This is bad! The cloud will cause an infectious condition for the human beings. I knew this would happen someday, but not now! I need to find a cure or they're going to accuse me, stake me. My kind cannot be extinct. The humankind is over, the cloud will spread country to country and all you will remember is the black cloud...

Maira Lakshmy Ratnarajah (12)
St George's School For Girls, Edinburgh

Contaminated

I wiped the ominous sweat off my forehead, I was close to death. My friend, my companion was now hunting me, was now thirsty for my blood. I'd lost so much. "Arghhhhh!"
Bang! My body, motionless, fell to the ground. A gun, I had never seen one before, but I couldn't daydream, I needed to focus. I could see a figure slowly approaching me. I had an urge to shoot and run, run and not look back. But I couldn't. Would I save a life of a mutant that was contaminated with the disease or would I kill and run?

Samantha Emson
St George's School For Girls, Edinburgh

The Fog

It had been a fortnight since I left my house. Provisions were low, and in order to get food, I would need to go outside. I walked towards the door, grabbed the metal handle and slowly opened it. I stood there, horrified at what I just had witnessed. I saw people lying on the ground, they lay there motionless. Their skin was blank, white like a canvas abandoned by their painter. There was no trace of colour on their faces, and their eyes, their pupils, stared into nothingness. Everyone was dead. But worst of all, I saw the fog coming...

Gabriela Wysocka (12)
St George's School For Girls, Edinburgh

Too Late?

The cure had to be here somewhere, but then it couldn't because I had pulled out every drawer and ripped open every cupboard. I could hear the breaths behind me, getting slower and slower each second. Why had I been picked for this job and why hadn't I been told where the cures were? The only thing in this room was paperwork upon paperwork. The breaths were getting slower. But then I remembered the room next door and there it was, lying wide open. I squished the purply-pink liquid into her mouth, but was it too late for her?

Charlotte Duffin (12)
St George's School For Girls, Edinburgh

My Loss

The last drop of blood fell from the person I most love, my only child, my daughter the last youngster alive on Earth. She's dead. There are no children left. Nobody can make another baby; nobody knows if there will ever be a cure. Which creature will be next? Why this now? What started it? Is the world coming to an end? I hear a deafening explosion. I hear people screaming and crying. I feel a chilling shiver down my spine. The door creaks then slowly slides open. Is it the after blast of the explosion or is something there?

Lindsay Young
St George's School For Girls, Edinburgh

The Cure

"The cure has to be here somewhere," I say to myself as I search the labs. Red lumps shoot up my arm, heading for my heart. I was told the cure was in a small tube with white pills. The problem is all the white pills are in small tubes. Suddenly, texts flood onto my phone. Each one is telling me a different detail. Orangey-yellow cap, black tube. I find the pills, but is it too late? My eyes are blurring up and my body loses strength. As I lift the pill towards my mouth, it slips out of my hand...

Lucy Gray (13)
St George's School For Girls, Edinburgh

Sinking

The giant, poisonous cloud fixed in the sky was spewing out a storm. The sea was crashing against the boat, effortlessly bringing it down. I could feel my feet starting to sting from the cold puddle I was standing in. There was no way out. I was on my own, stranded, defeated. The boat was quickly filling up now, sinking into the darkness below me. The water was up to my chest now, all I could do was swim, but where? Where could I go when all I could see were grey clouds and a dark, monstrous sea below me?

Alice Honley (15)
St George's School For Girls, Edinburgh

Being Infected

People dropping by the minute… Two days before when I was young, my mum told me a story about the world ending, I never thought that it would come true. It was a normal Monday until I saw the victim hurry out of class. I was so scared after school finished. I ran out, everyone was killing each other. I was petrified. I tried calling my mum, it was too late. My mum was biting my shoulder, blood dripping, but then I felt something scuttling under my skin and I tried to get it out, but it was too late…

Esmé Drummond (12)
St George's School For Girls, Edinburgh

The Last Dance

My skin felt burning like I was being flayed. Around twelve hours ago, my feet had started to tap and my arms, my legs and my head had started to wave. I could not stop dancing. Exhaustion and hunger had eaten away at me. I couldn't stop. Every time I had tried, my body erupted in pain. My heart screamed in protest as it slowed down, about to stop. The doctors had told me what would happen if I stopped, my heart would cease to beat and I would die. As I flailed, so did the wires making me move.

Rebecca Tidswell (12)
St George's School For Girls, Edinburgh

The Scratcher

Something scuttled under my skin and it felt slimy and gooey and I didn't know what it was. Suddenly, I felt it nipping, scratching, ripping and tearing my skin. I turned my head and what did I see? I saw blood, big bits of drippy blood. It was dripping off my arm and falling to the ground. There was a huge puddle of it. Then I was screaming in pain and in fear. I peered at my arm and I saw this brown, long creature scuttling out of my arm. I had no idea what it was. I was terrified.

Morgan Matthews (11)
St George's School For Girls, Edinburgh

Crawler

"C'mon Sarah!"

I was sitting there, blood on my skin, the knife in my trembling hand, waiting for supplies.

"Max, stop scream- oh my God, I'll get bandages."

I brought the knife to the back of my neck, trying desperately to remove the microchip, the thing that made the Crawlers.

"Sarah, it's not my blood. It's Crawler blood," I said, calmly.

"Crawler! Max, are you okay?"

"Sarah, pass over the gun and don't move. There, behind you!"

She was turning into one.

"Kill me."

She kicked the gun over. I had to choose. Kill Sarah or the Crawlers... *Bang!*

"Goodbye."

Kai Dark (12)
St Machar Academy, Aberdeen

The End

Bang! Europeans were doomed, Americans victorious. The continent felt icy-cold for the few who lived. The bodies lay still like time had stopped, looking as pale as the surrounding dust. The living had nothing. Food contaminated, water contaminated, air contaminated. The survivors were few. The atomic bomb hit Frankfurt and nobody nearer than St Petersburg or Monte Carlo wasn't suffering.

"America is victorious! Colossal in victory! Europe was destroyed, wrecked, as dusty as a sandstorm. Trees still, grass depressed and lifeless, bodies dead with numbers in the millions!" roared the journalist.

The question is, how would the living survive?

Ben Thom (13)
St Machar Academy, Aberdeen

War Against The Martians

"Markus... Markus... wake up!" cried Claudia. "Doctor, can't you do anything? He's suffering really bad from the poison dart."

"Damn those Martians," said Felix angrily.

At this rate, there would only be three survivors left: Felix, Claudia and Dr Dare. Right now, the humans were at a crusade between the Martians and the Martians were wiping out the human race. There were not many survivors.

"Quick, the Martians are infiltrating us!" screamed Dr Dare.

"What's the point? This war is like a maze and now we've met our dead end," Markus replied.

Sadly, they were his last words...

Leya Shaju (12)
St Machar Academy, Aberdeen

The Bright Light

"OMG! We're nearly there?" moaned Ami.
"Should be around the corner..." mumbled Kai.
They pulled in at the side of the road.
"Where even are we?" Shannon said angrily.
Suddenly, a light, brighter than the sun, flashed deep in the dark forest behind them. The light grew bigger and passed by them. Their bodies turned cold as ice, their eyes went pure white, they quickly fell to the ground and had a seizure. Their hearts stopped beating and their blood stopped pumping... they were dead. But it wasn't just them... the light spread and the whole of humanity was doomed!

Sinead Mayo Conlon (13)
St Machar Academy, Aberdeen

The End Of Us

"It's been three years since the horrific effects of the war began. The final nuke that was fired by the UK landed in the centre of Iran, unleashing the last of the deadly smallpox disease. The disease rapidly evolved, combining with the radiation... there was no hope for humanity," monologued Sam in a dark corner of the bunker.

"Oh, shut up!" whined Sally, Sam's considerably saner sister. "We'll be out of this hellhole soon." Suddenly, the bunker roof opened up and a bloodied corpse fell into the bunker. There was no hope for humanity now - or was there?

Euan Reid (12)
St Machar Academy, Aberdeen

Rat Invasion

"Quick, run!" someone screamed.
There were rats everywhere, well, they looked like rats. I'd never seen them before, I don't think anyone had, but the gross creatures were biting everyone, making them fall quickly to the floor. Everyone was dying. I just kept running. The 'rats' were right behind me, fifty of them: brutal, brown, black. Tails the length of my finger. That's when I decided I wasn't going to get away. One by one the 'rats' sank their yellow teeth into my ankle. I fell to the ground. My body went numb. Slowly, my eyes filled with darkness.

Gemma Still (12)
St Machar Academy, Aberdeen

Humanity

"Day 64: I believe I'm the only one left. The vile Anti-men have taken everyone: friends, family. I only have Sparky: my dog. I've decided to let myself be taken too so I could save my family."
"I looked out the window and saw Anti-men in Hazmat suits. I'm currently hiding as I speak on this recorder. I hear footsteps and weird, electronic voices. I don't understand them. I'm going to keep recording."
"Get out, Joey! You've been contaminated by humanity. We have a cure."
The electronic voices command and I follow.

Oliwia Wilkosz (13)
St Machar Academy, Aberdeen

The Unthinkable

We finally emerged from under the bunker. They had got us. They had spread this disease around, which looked highly contagious. Everyone was fading, everyone just dropped dead.
Red rashes were appearing on our legs. We were the only ones left. This rash started evolving on our bodies. Before it was fire, now there was nothing. Everyone had changed. Everything was different. We didn't know what to do or where to go. It was terrifying. I had a panic attack, everything happened so quickly. I was fine with them. Just the fact that there was nothing left. Nothing at all.

Drew Kris McDermid (14)
St Machar Academy, Aberdeen

Race To Antarctica

Patient 0 lay on the ground, helpless. Four weeks in: we hadn't been able to find a cure to this mystifying disease. Now, the first reported case had died. What next for Earth's inhabitants? Three days on, the population of the Earth had dropped: very few had survived. Those who had raced to the only known part of the world where the disease was unable to survive: Antarctica. With all the ice caps melting, Antarctica couldn't contain the human race. Besides, no one had lived in Antarctica without being expertly trained. What next for Earth inhabitants?

Sol Bewley-Lataix (13)
St Machar Academy, Aberdeen

Just Give Up

It happened on TV. *Boom!* Most of the human race was infected and perished from seizures. Only a handful were immune. The uninfected had to disentangle this mystery.

They didn't know why they were uninfected or who caused it, but the hunt began. To make sure nothing was in the air, they wore peculiar masks. The infected were after them so they had to act fast.

Three left and no advancement, but they found that if you were touched, you became infected. No food or water, they were giving up. Later, they were cornered and gave up to the contamination...

Noah Jack (12)
St Machar Academy, Aberdeen

Deadly Virus

There has been a virus that has spread across the world. It spread from someone that had an infection, anything that the person touched was infected. People were saying it was the end of the world. Eventually, it would kill everyone. It had already killed 25% of humanity. People had locked themselves in their houses, locked the doors and windows and wouldn't let anyone in or out. Schools had shut, teachers and pupils were trapped in the schools. If you went outside, you'd be dead. But if you didn't, you'd eventually starve to death. Who would survive?

Kaitlyn Ellis-Jones (12)
St Machar Academy, Aberdeen

The Mission

The rash was spreading, pulsing, hurting. Everyone turned into zombies, there were only a couple of people left. They didn't know what to do, they didn't have much time left. The monsters were looking for the people and they were so close to finding them. The people had to make a really quick plan before they were caught. If they didn't make a quick plan, Earth would be full of viruses and monsters. The humans did have a really good hiding place, but they couldn't stay there forever... The question was, what would they do, would Earth be normal again?

Natalia Skowronek (12)
St Machar Academy, Aberdeen

The Fear Of Death Is Unavoidable

It's been three months since we escaped the church of Satan. Me, Lily and James unfolded the end of the world. We later learned the church was connected to a higher source. They controlled humans through music, making people objects, creatures not human. Lily's eyes black, tearing with blood... Her soul slowly being drained from her body. Anyone affected seems to still have a mind of their own, they know *exactly* what they're doing. Yet, somehow, we are untouched. *What if James and I are the only ones immune, but how? Why us? Why now?*

Zeniya Elaine Pantcheva (14)
St Machar Academy, Aberdeen

All Human?

I walked back into the house where I faced my family. The day had finally arrived where we were the only ones left. We were expecting this. The plan, made hundreds of years ago by our family, had succeeded. Everyone was wiped out by an 'airborne' disease that spread rapidly. Now was our chance to bring the rest of our kind here. Earth was finally how it should've been: no humans, dozens of new technologies and a new species! Aliens were as smart as the three smartest beings combined, but were they really smart enough to wipe out all human?

Leah Paterson (13)
St Machar Academy, Aberdeen

Water Of Annihilation

Everyone is gone. No one is here. It seems I am the lone survivor in this ravaged land. The main cause of this tragedy was one drop of acid. But this lone drop was enough to eradicate almost all living creatures. This calamity, which erased the Earth of all entities, occurred when the tainted government put deadly toxins in all of the Earth's water reserves, slowly poisoning human cultivation. Those who dwelled whilst poisoned instantaneously perished, *boom!* Dropped like flies. What is the point in existing if I can abolish it all now?

Brandon Lee Booth (13)
St Machar Academy, Aberdeen

Deadly Disease

Instantly, everyone that had the disease had to be evacuated. Immediately, Africa's population was decreasing rapidly. First contact with this disease was like being struck by deadly lightning. My mother caught the disease a few weeks ago. I was crying. She had to go to the research centre to test for a cure.

I hope she will be okay. The scientists are saying that the disease is everywhere in the air and there is no way to cure it. All of my friends have caught the disease and I might have to travel to another country for treatment.

Michael Claro (13)
St Machar Academy, Aberdeen

My Monster Infection

Just 387 people are left alive in the UK and all this is happening because of infection. The infection makes people like monsters or dangerous animals. These monsters are really dangerous, they're killing people and if they hurt someone, the person becomes the same as the monsters. People try to find something that can help, but nothing helps and every day people are still dying or changing to monsters. People even try to kill them, but it doesn't work. They just lose a lot of lives, but police try to save as many people as they can.

Dana Pinkovska (12)
St Machar Academy, Aberdeen

The Ice Glacier

The ice glacier melted. Water rushed through the land, leaving Canada the only country above water. We looked for people who might be approaching a water source that wasn't contaminated with chemicals. We found a dam and people. The dam wasn't contaminated, we were saved.

Twenty years later, we were nearly out of water and 10,000 people left alive. *Crack!* Something broke in the dam, scientists were trying to make water from hydrogen and oxygen but there wasn't enough hydrogen or oxygen to survive and make water!

Jorge Lama (13)
St Machar Academy, Aberdeen

The Invasion

It was just a normal school day when I was in class. Me and my friends heard something, it was zombies. We barricaded the door and windows and armed ourselves with pencils sharp as needles. The zombies smashed down the door. Me and my friends attacked. We managed to kill them but, unfortunately, we didn't know the real horror that was going on a couple of days before the attack. There were reports of green clouds over all the other continents. There was no more news from them and when we looked outside, there were green clouds...

Hadyn Milne (13)
St Machar Academy, Aberdeen

End Of Life

Boom! An explosion in the air, birds falling from the sky. Fish floating in the river. Human beings were getting sick, it had a big impact in the UK. Almost the whole population was dead. I saw something in the sky, it seemed to be a rocket ship. It was dashing down really quick. It started getting closer to me, then it crashed. I heard footsteps coming closer to me, I heard someone speaking in a weird language. I didn't recognise the language. I was fading out of consciousness. I looked in the sky. A green cloud...?

John Ogston (12)
St Machar Academy, Aberdeen

Parasitic Creatures

I've been sitting here for months, I haven't heard anything from the outside. I feel like there is no one left but me. I have a radio, I am trying to find something. Nothing. I've been running out of food, worrying that I will have to go out.
The other night, I was sound asleep. I felt something crawling on my hand. I felt a sharp sting, I sprang out of bed. I saw the parasitic creature crawling inside my skin. I rushed for my knife and cut it out in time. I bandaged it up and calmed myself down...

Amanda Suprowicz (13)
St Machar Academy, Aberdeen

The Final Four

It had been almost a thousand years since the deathly affliction had vanished, but there was something that the humankind didn't know. They didn't know that it was coming back. It all started in Egypt. The affliction carrier, a rat, bit a little girl. She carried it through her family, through Egypt, through the whole world! Everyone died, except four people who were hiding in their underground bunker. When they emerged, everyone around them was dead. They knew there was no way of bringing them back.

Auguste Urbonaite (12)
St Machar Academy, Aberdeen

The Last Survivors

As Dr Bobby walked past, the creature's vault cracked. He ignored it. *Bang!* He turned at the speed of light to the sight of a razor exuding blood. He saw a doctor on the floor. They were the last survivors. Madness unravelled right in front of his eyes. He saw his own mum perish into thin air. He heard the howl from the dust storm outside and the creature getting closer. He needed to reproduce and quick. But it was a risk. He took the gamble, it was a risk. He got caught. Humanity gone…

Suriya Sivakumar (12)
St Machar Academy, Aberdeen

A Frozen World

I gazed out the window at the icy desert. An angry wind blew fiercely. Two weeks ago, scientists found a fast-growing ice that spread and brought a disease that wiped out most of humanity. If the cold and disease didn't get you, they would. The world was like a frozen hell. Then I saw the face of a boy. I fell backwards in shock. I got up and had a look at him. He looked strangely familiar. Curiously, I opened the window. *Gasp!* I couldn't believe it. It was him. He was alive...

Katie Watson (13)
St Machar Academy, Aberdeen

June 1st, 3099

The human race is dying. I think I'm the only one left in my city or even my country. I can't go outside. It's going to wipe me out as well. It's a big wind that circles you and it's impossible to get out of. I've watched many people get wiped out by the wind that's as dark as night and it howls. What is it? I've heard screams coming from the wind. I want to help them but I'm too scared to die. Soon, I'll have to go out, I won't live any longer...

Abbie Ann Shepherd (12)
St Machar Academy, Aberdeen

The Deadly Disease

Something scuttled under my skin. I woke up. I was cold. I curled up in a ball, scared and alone. I decided to get up and try. I'm in an underground bunker. I looked around for something, maybe an idea? Something to help me not get the disease. I was one of the only survivors left: the human race had died. Then I heard three knocks on the door. I wasn't alone... who was it? Did they have the disease? Was I going to get the disease if I opened the door? Was I going to live or die?

Chloe Fyfe (12)
St Machar Academy, Aberdeen

Mutation America

Dr Palmer is the last person in America. If he can't find a cure, then America is doomed. The last drop went into the test tube like a weeping soul. Dr Palmer felt successful, then the unthinkable happened. DNA mutation had reached the lab. Dr Palmer tried the cure, it worked. Now Dr Palmer needed to find a way to distribute it across America so people could become normal again. Dr Palmer put the cure in a sprayer. People slowly became normal. Dr Palmer did it. He saved America.

Morgan Glennie (13)
St Machar Academy, Aberdeen

Poison

The last drop fell into the test tube, he mixed the wrong liquid. We gave it to the doctor to give to ill people but the liquid was stuff that could kill you. It was handed to ill people who wanted it and that was a lot of people. Sadly, everyone that took it died. There was no way you would survive it so it spread around the whole world. It would never stop going, it would start going to different countries and everyone was going to die sadly. It would not ever stop!

Cameron Stewart (12)
St Machar Academy, Aberdeen

Can It Be True?

Me and my friend were in my dad's lab when we heard, "Run!"
Mikey shouted, "What is it?"
"Zombies!" my dad yelled.
So we ran upstairs to the window, we saw 100 zombies. They got my dad so I grabbed a shotgun. We killed 99 zombies, hoping the last one was my dad! We decimated him and it... was my dad! My family was so happy we had him back. I never left his side because of that day. I was as happy as a dog with a treat.

Billy Swan (13)
St Machar Academy, Aberdeen

No More Mercy!

Five years after the nuclear war, I woke up. It was the middle of the night. Screams were as loud as a shop on a Saturday morning. Only ten of us left. In our shelter, history was repeating itself. Dinosaurs! We had thirty-one women and seven men. We tried to get babies but every pregnancy went down to suffering and then death. We didn't have much time left. The bunker was like an Arctic winter, we were losing energy and food. Could we survive? God, help us!

Kuba Szelagowski (13)
St Machar Academy, Aberdeen

The Unknown Contamination

There were soldiers and doctors everywhere, helping people. Well, that's how it was in the beginning. Now, there are barely any of us left and food is definitely running out. The people that were with me were Lewis and Paul. Nobody that we have come across knows how the world's population of humans dropped so drastically. Still, the scariest thing was walking down the street and having to look at all the bodies lying there, lifeless.

Milan Bogacki (12)
St Machar Academy, Aberdeen

Alien Invasion

It was a dark and foggy night with a bright green-red light. I saw a light shadow. It did not look familiar and all I heard was the door slamming. Stomping up the stairs, up to my room. It was an alien. They covered me with their green slime and now have taken over all of the human race and the whole world. Who knew if someone was still out there in the dead, slimy world, and what was going to happen next? Who was still alive?

Erin McDonald (13)
St Machar Academy, Aberdeen

Killing The World

"Sir..."
"What is it now?"
"Test Subject A6 is missing"
"Which one is that again?"
"The infected one."
"Well, what are you waiting for? Go and find her!"
"Sir, we have searched the whole building. She isn't here, besides she could have killed the whole state by now."
"Do I have to do everything around here?"
"Sorry, sir."
"You are gonna need to call them."
"I'm on it, sir."
"Thank you, now get out of here."
"Yes sir."
The man rushed away down the long eerie corridor...

Hayley Robinson (12)
Stirling High School, Stirling

The Cure

"The cure has to be around here somewhere," said Caroline.
Caroline scattered all through the old dusty books. Then all of a sudden, *crack!*
"Ah-ha!"
"Hey, what's going on in there?" said an old grumpy man.
Caroline started to run inside the secret room to try to find her way out. As she looked back she saw the man chasing after her. Caroline was filled with fear but managed to find an exit which was locked!
"Hey, get back here!"
Caroline quickly ducked and hid under a desk, waiting for her key to freedom.

Abbie Barjoti (12)
Stirling High School, Stirling

Tester 13

Italy, Rome 1974
"Today on BBC, a Tester from the Colosseum Science lab has escaped, the Tester 13 has a hallucination virus, stay safe."
Rome 1978
I was walking through the abandoned city. Every step echoed, I felt I was being watched, a street light flickered... I felt my weight give way dropping to the floor, I felt my heart slow down, my scream echoed down the street. I turned, staring the killer in the face, it was a dark figure with a ghost white face wielding a knife, I recognized the face.
"Mum..."
A smirk crossed the killer's face.

Ella Caitlin Dempsey (12)
Stirling High School, Stirling

Omnic Crisis

June 9th 2078

Robots have become self-aware and have attacked the human race. What's left of us are hiding in domes made by the government.

July 2nd

We're close to making an EMP bomb powerful enough to wipe out the full east coast, only a few days left until the world's safe and we don't have to stay here.

September 1st

The government's given the location of us to the omnics/robots, time to see if the EMP works, if not we're dead.

An hour later...

Everyone's dead, not me. I'm the last one left, I won't make it out alive...

George MacLean (12)
Stirling High School, Stirling

Mysterious White Powder

The high-pitched screeching flooded my ears, filling me with a deep pain. My body shook, as I heard more families scream for help. Though no one could. If one had been touched by the mysterious white powder, they instantly become infected. We were an abundant colony, going about our daily business, and now this. Another screech filled my body, every one more haunting than the last. We had no idea what this white, smoky powder thing was. Why was it here? The only evidence we had was a small square-shaped object that said *Ant Killer*.

Scarlett Roy (12)
Stirling High School, Stirling

The Death Of Humanity

It was intended to be a cure for cancer code-named Project C. It ended up going horribly wrong and the scientists created a disease worse than cancer that would leave the people infected dead in a week. The scientists simply wrote it off as a failure and went home for the day, but then, a week later, the police found them dead. They were confused and left, but little did they know they had caught the deadly disease which then started to spread from person to person. This disease grew to kill almost all the people on Earth.

Stephen Kerr (12)
Stirling High School, Stirling

They're Coming...

As I emerged from my bunker I could see all of my friends lying on the ground infected and soon started to cry.
"I must carry on before they find me," I said to myself.
As I started to walk away, I felt someone breathing on my shoulder, it was at that moment that I realised that I was being followed, so, being my usual curious self, I turned around to see who was there, but no one was there. So I turned back around, but as soon as I turned around, I realised they were following me from behind me...

Chloe Charlotte Stark (12)
Stirling High School, Stirling

Zombie Apocalypse

It has been fifteen hours since we found out about the zombie apocalypse. The apocalypse has started. Me and my family all ran to our farmhouse to get the guns. *Bang bang!* The zombies are banging at all the doors. As I pull back the cupboard to reveal the gun store, three zombies enter our house. My mum and dad grab a gun as quick as they can and shoot all three zombies that entered before they can get any closer. We all get guns and head into my grandad's van. My dad starts the van and we are off...

Kyle Saunders (12)
Stirling High School, Stirling

The Girl

Fear rose up my spine. I had a vision of a woman running away from a tall building. I could have sworn it was 'her'. Time stilled at that moment. Cries for help were coming from outside. I grabbed my mask and I ran. My friends... dead. Their bodies... cold and lifeless. I tripped and fell onto the concrete ground, stunned by the life I no longer have. My mask fell from my face. I didn't have the strength to get up. Blackness was all I could see. I rose up and glared down. I wish I never saw that...

Jenifer June Gillespie (12)
Stirling High School, Stirling

The Cloud

Families were ripped apart due to a tiny virus, Greyscale. The virus made the victim see the world in greyscale, then the person's skin would dry and go a foul grey colour and it would resemble scales and when the scales came that infected area would become paralysed. The scales would spread until the whole body was almost stone-like. And I had a cure. I was about to give it to someone, the only phial of cure in the world. My hand caught greyscale and it started to fall. Was this the end of humanity?

Archie West (12)
Stirling High School, Stirling

Don't Look

There's no way to survive. If we look, we will die. There is no way of escaping this. We must stay indoors. We can never go outside again. I can't see anyone but all I can hear is screaming, car crashes, gunshots and the sound of suicide. There is a flash of silence. No one to be heard. I am the only person alive. If I don't leave soon, I will starve. If I leave there is a chance I won't come back. It's here! The only option is death. I look and there's nothing I can do about it.

Melissa Turnbull (12)
Stirling High School, Stirling

Ever-Spreading

The ground around me turned black. Anything touching the rotten ground was lowering down and disappearing. The ground was slowly turning to black sinking sand. Everyone was running in all directions, I just stood there, frozen in fear.
I heard a sudden cry, "Emma, run!"
So I obeyed, I sprinted randomly until a thought hit me. I was paralysed in my own mind. The ever-spreading black ground was heading slowly towards the nursery. I knew it was too late to save him, my brother!

Alyssa Nash (14)
Stirling High School, Stirling

Rush Hour

Rush hour is at 5pm, it lasts for an hour and this is when the whole town has to hide or run to get away from this sort of monster. We call it the runner, and if you get too close it will brainwash you and it will do something horrible. Sometimes you won't make it, sometimes you get hurt badly, though I am one of the few people alive. But it won't last that long in my head, I am living in a factory basement with two other people. The food is running out, will we survive?

Lauren Graham (12)
Stirling High School, Stirling

YOUNG WRITERS INFORMATION

We hope you have enjoyed reading this book – and that you will continue to in the coming years.

If you're a young writer who enjoys reading and creative writing, or the parent of an enthusiastic poet or story writer, do visit our website **www.youngwriters.co.uk**. Here you will find free competitions, workshops and games, as well as recommended reads, a poetry glossary and our blog.

If you would like to order further copies of this book, or any of our other titles, then please give us a call or order via your online account.

Young Writers
Remus House
Coltsfoot Drive
Peterborough
PE2 9BF
(01733) 890066
info@youngwriters.co.uk

Join in the conversation!

 YoungWritersUK   @YoungWritersCW